I'm Isabell Monk

as told to Caren B. Stelson

Celebration Press
Parsippany, New Jersey

I'm Isabell Monk. I write books for children. But that's not how I started out.

I started out as a kid, just like you. Looking back, I was a very lucky kid.

I was lucky because I had
Mrs. Upshaw.

4

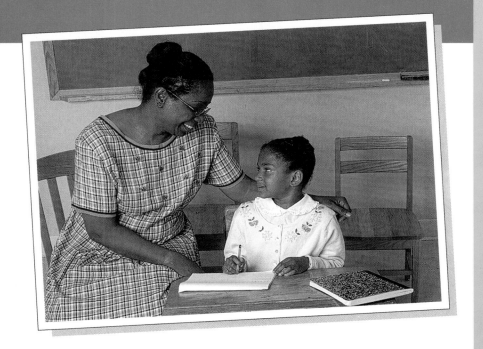

Mrs. Upshaw was my first grade
teacher. She called me her little
dumpling. Then she taught me
how to write. I didn't know what
I'd been missing!

You see, before I went to school, I didn't know how to write. I didn't know I could write.

Mrs. Upshaw changed all that.
She said writing was amazing.
She showed me how little circles
and lines could turn into letters.
Those letters could turn into
words. And those words could
turn into stories.

Mrs. Upshaw believed in me. She
wanted to know my ideas. She
wanted to know what I cared
about. She wanted me to write
about all those things. She
wanted me to tell my stories.

Isabell acting in a play

I liked to write, but I also liked to act. I wanted to make stories come alive on stage. When I grew up, that's just what I did.

Then one night I had a dream about a little girl. Her mama was black. Her papa was white. I wanted her always to be proud. In my dream her name was Hope.

When I woke up, I knew I had a story to tell. I wrote it down fast. I could see Mrs. Upshaw smiling and saying, "Keep writing, Isabell."

I worked hard writing my story.
I made change after change.

When I thought my story sounded just right, I printed a copy out. I sent it to an editor at a publishing company.

Then one day I got a phone call from the editor. She said she wanted to make my story into a book! We worked together to do just that.

Do you know what? Mrs. Upshaw was right. Writing is amazing!

When I write, I can share my dreams with you. I can share my feelings, hopes, and ideas. What could you share with me?